Copyright © Helen I Ogilvie 2023
Published 2023
Layout design by team effort
Cover photo source unknown

All rights reserved. No part of this publication may be reproduced, stored in a retrieval system or transmitted in any form by any means; electronic, mechanical, photocopying, recording or otherwise, without the prior permission of the publisher / author, unless specified.

Ogilvie, Helen I, 1947 —
Broken Chains: I once was bound … but now I'm free

1. Reflective Poetry   2. Prayers   3. Devotions   I. Title

ISBN: 978-0-646-87626-9
Digital images used and modified with permission.
Illustrations by Sophie and Alicia Ogilvie.

Published by Helen I Ogilvie
Berwick, VICTORIA 3806
hiogilvie3@gmail.com

Acknowledgements

Gary Lewis for his patience, understanding and help.

Sophie and Alicia — my Grand Daughters — for their amazing illustrations.

Ps Michael Rojales for his encouragement.

Index

In the Beginning p6
- Creation
- The Potter
- God's Wonder
- The New Believer

Transformation p11
- God's Forgiveness
- Grace and Mercy
- Trust
- Liberation
- Blindness
- Freedom
- Thankyou

Anxious Times p19
- Covid
- My Storm
- Sleepless Nights
- Put God First
- Let Go and Let God

God's Protection p26
- Always
- Jesus
- God's Care
- Honour
- Peace

God's Purpose p31
- Understanding
- Your Plan
- The Holy Spirit
- Possessions
- Our Greatest Aim
- Here is my Heart

Prayer and Encouragement p38
- Opening Prayer
- A Close Friend has Died
- Reach Out
- Encouraging Others
- I Want …
- Fruits of The Spirit
- Send Me

Grief p47
- A Mother's Love
- A Lost Son
- Every Day
- Different Paths

Reflections p51
- The Past
- Repentance

Gratitude p54
- My Cup
- Providence
- God's Grace
- My Guide
- To Know You
- Perfect Match
- Grand Children

God's Victory p62
- Standing in His Victory
- God's Mercy
- I Surrender
- My Lord and Saviour
- Looking Back

Introduction

I write from my heart.
Words pop into my head at inconvenient times...
at night, when shopping, exercising or driving.
I write them down, knowing they are from God

My Grand Daughters, Sophie and Alicia, illustrated this book.
Each inspired and blessed me.
My gratitude for their wonderful contributions.

All proceeds from this book will go to support
the work of Missions, through
Berwick Church of Christ,
Melbourne.

In the Beginning

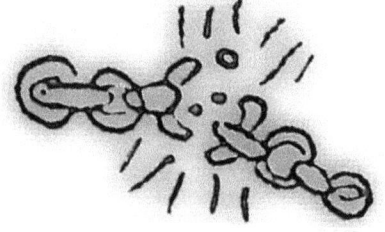

Creation

This world was made at Your command ...
perfection, beauty; all You planned.
The light and dark, the hills and dales,
the sky and sea... such fine details.
All creatures, nature, fish and birds
appeared when You said three powerful words ...
"Let there be" ... and then there was!
Creation, stunning and without flaws.
Oh, God, we bow our heads to say
our thank You for our world today.

IN THE BEGINNING

The Potter

God's the Potter, I'm the clay.
He shapes me, moulds me, day by day.
His loving hands surround my life ...
He strengthens me through good and strife.

His Potter's hands perfect my being ...
through different eyes I am now seeing.
I thank You, Lord, for changing me ...
I thank You, Lord, that I now see.

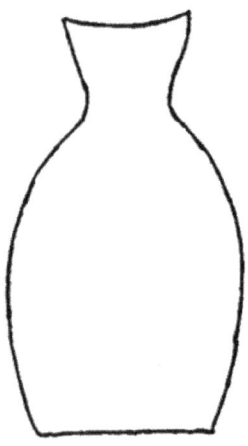

God's Wonder

God, glorious and wonderful ...
Heavenly Father, powerful.
I am but a grain of sand
so grateful for Your guiding hand.
Grant me wisdom, day by day,
as I kneel to You and pray.
I thank You, Lord, for Your great love
and all Your blessings from above.

In the Beginning

New Believer

Oh, Jesus; You have held me close
since the day that I was born.
Despite my sin, You cherished me ...
undeserving and forlorn.

For years I never understood
that You watched over me.
But, when I felt The Holy Spirit
my eyes opened ... I could see.

I always used to rush around,
fulfil my selfish will.
Since knowing You and loving You
I pray, I wait, I'm still.

There are times You've rocked my boat
and sometimes tipped me out!
But You caught me in Your loving arms
and changed my life about.

Your timing's always been spot on
as I now reflect... and see
the forgiveness, grace, peace and love
You showered over me.

I thank You for my life on earth,
Your hand guiding me through.
I'm blessed and loved, my future is
eternity with You.

Transformation

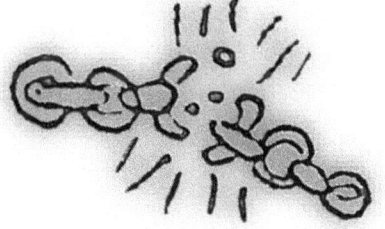

TRANSFORMATION

God's Forgiveness

Thank You, Lord, for Your forgiveness;
thank You, Lord, for changing me.
I've been released from all my chains ...
Your love and grace have set me free.

I'm on my knees with gratitude ...
my sins forgiven, my future sound.
Dear Jesus, in these challenging times
I know all answers in You are found.

I walk with You, I talk with You ...
when I'm tempted ... I hear Your voice.
You convict me ... gently, quietly ...
I turn, obey; that's now my choice.

Thank You, Lord, for being my shield and
for being my refuge, too.
Knowing You has changed my life ...
I now surrender all to You.

Grace and Mercy

God has drowned me in His grace
and I can now stand tall.
I close my eyes and see His face ...
He'll be there when I fall.

He never fails, His plan is true,
His timing ... always right.
He's nurtured me since I was young ...
He knew I'd see the light.

The peace and love I feel each day,
when I hear His voice.
I know God's there, He hears me pray ...
in His comfort I rejoice.

I'm filled with His love and grace,
I know I can't go wrong ... because
His blessings and forgiveness
just go on and on, and on.

Transformation

Trust

Jesus, I stand before You now
    in humility and awe.
For years I did life on my own ...
    I struggled on, so sure.

My life's been full of ups and downs ...
    I left You ... then returned.
The highs and lows and roundabouts
    have often left me burned.

I've lived in cold, dark places
    where I could not see ...
but You found me every time
    and You've hung on to me.

I've reached my three score years and ten,
    so blessed I've seen the light.
I'm trying to live a worthy life ...
    honourable in Your sight.

Liberation

Jesus, I confess all my sin
committed in my youth.
My chains and shame now gone from me
because I've learned Your truth.

I'm not proud of some things I've done
when spiritually empty.
I knew Your name, but not Your love ...
that's changed, I now have plenty.

You rescued me, You carried me ...
You left the 99.
I felt Your touch, repented ...
and now I know You're mine.

I am human, I still sin
but acknowledge now my faults.
Your patience, Lord, is endless and
it's You whom I exalt.

Blindness

Lord, I was blind ... refused to see
my life's purpose is in You.
Lead me to others whose eyes are closed
so they can know You, too.

Your love, forgiveness, mercy, grace and
humility have no bounds.
Your gentle voice keeps guiding me
since You turned my life around.

I've been tipped out of many boats
in my younger, selfish past.
But I know You always caught me and
into Your arms I passed.

I was in the wilderness when
You gently touched my soul.
I felt Your strength and comfort
and since then I've been made whole.

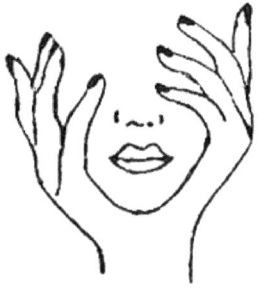

Freedom

Self-condemnation haunts me
and dominates my being.
When I recall its origins
I don't like what I'm seeing.

God's grace and mercy cover me ...
I prayed to be released
from all the pain, the hurt and shame
poured on me by the beast.

I know that I'm Your daughter
and You've long forgiven me;
there's no place for my guilt and shame,
Jesus' blood set me free.

I renounce the enemy's strongholds,
negativity and lies.
No longer am I blinded
as I see through Godly eyes.

I refuse to live in fear,
be overpowered or controlled.
The enemy has no place here
as God's name I uphold.

I will live in the grace and mercy,
and freedom that He's given.
Thank You for Your protection, Lord,
which covers me from Heaven.

Thankyou

Y ou changed me from the inside out
when I was born again.
My life, different in every way,
between now and then.

I have sinned but now repent,
I'm trying to do more good.
Reflecting now, I clearly see
I didn't love You as I should.

I thank You, Lord, for shaping me
through every selfish choice.
I remember well the awesome day
when I heard Your gentle voice.

With joyful hope I felt renewed ...
my life's direction changed.
Oh Jesus, thank You for Your touch,
I'm completely rearranged.

ANXIOUS TIMES

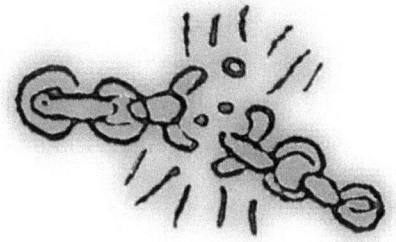

Covid

The Covid cloud descended and filled our world with fear.
No routine, friends or family ... oh God, show us You're here.

Our lives just stopped, or so it seemed; an unbelievable change.
We comforted, we zoomed and walked; God help us find our range.

Endless lockdowns ... what's happening? We can't go on this way!
Anger and uncertainty affect us every day.

Some cope well ... others don't ... anxiety is rife.
I pray for wisdom and patience, Lord, that You transcend my life.

This stop-start life is challenging ... it's hard to live this way.
My focus and my purpose gone ... I need You, Lord, each day.

As Your blessed sons and daughters we thank You, oh so much.
We love You and we trust You, God, and feel Your precious touch.

We know that You are with us and this season will soon leave ...
please grant strength and wisdom to all those who believe.

The Covid cloud's still with us but we no longer fear.
We know Your plan is perfect and we know that You are here.

My Storm

In the midst of my storm I know You are here
guiding my every move.
In the midst of my storm I don't have any fear,
I know You have nothing to prove.

I trust in You, Lord, that You'll bring me through
the challenges which I now face.
I trust in You, Lord, I know You are true
as I feel Your forgiveness and grace.

I worship and thank You for all that I am …
once broken but now I'm Your child.
I worship and thank You, God's Perfect Lamb,
I'm at peace and with You reconciled.

I want all my thoughts, my words and my deeds
to be Yours, channelled through me.
I want the whole world to bow down and believe
in You, the Saviour we need.

At the end of the day, I sit and reflect
on Your peace, Your blessings and love.
At the end of the day I know what to expect …
my future in Heaven, above.

Sleepless Nights

I sometimes lie awake at night
and worry floods my mind,
I turn to You and talk to You ...
Your words are soft and kind.

When I find it hard to sleep
and wonder how I'll cope ...
I tell You all that's going on ...
Your answers give me hope.

You guide me to the crossroads and
Your way becomes so clear.
You hold me and You walk with me
and I forget my fear.

Knowing that You're with me
fills me with certainty.
My trust in You is pure and strong
for all eternity.

Put God First

I need You in my life on earth
and love it when we talk.
But sometimes I don't put You first
and then ... alone I walk.

It's those times when I struggle
to keep my life on track.
I spiral down and wonder why
I'm under enemy attack.

Reality hits me again ...
Your forgiveness floods my soul.
You hold me tight ... I feel Your love ...
and once again I'm whole.

Let Go and Let God ...

When troubling thoughts and times appear
and you don't want to face your fear ...
let go and let God.

When you feel alone and wonder why
and you don't even want to try ...
let go and let God.

When you feel let down, misunderstood
or nothing you say is any good ...
let go and let God.

When hopelessness consumes your day
and you find it hard to pray ...
let go and let God.

When problems make your life so tough
and you believe you've had enough ...
let go and let God.

When desperation floods your life
and anguish cuts you like a knife ...
let go and let God.

Broken Chains

When the enemy comes to taunt
and guilt, and shame return to haunt ...
let go and let God.

When your future's looking bleak
forget those worldly things you seek ...
let go and let God.

Although your hope is growing dim
don't give up your trust in Him ...
let go and let God.

God's always with you, near and far ...
loving, guiding, wherever you are ... so,
let go and let God.

GOD'S PROTECTION

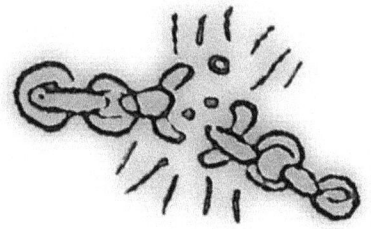

Always

I know You're always with me and
I know You'll always care.
I know You'll always prompt me
because You're always there.

Sometimes I don't listen and
sometimes I don't hear.
Sometimes I think I know best
and those sometimes lead to fear.

Please prompt me when I fail You;
please convict me every time.
Please forgive when I repent ...
You tell me that You're mine.

I want to be obedient and
I want to do Your will.
I want to honour You always ...
to sit with You and be still.

God's Protection

Jesus

With You, Lord, all things are possible ...
I marvel at Your ways.
You know my heart, my mind and thoughts,
and the number of my days.
You chose me and I followed You ...
You changed my life for good.
The guilt and sin from years long past
have gone ... never thought they would.

When young I was a captive,
a slave to worldly sin.
The idols of my un-Christian life
no longer live within.
You forgave me and You touched my heart,
after many misspent years.
I never want to let You down ...
I'm Yours and have no fears.

You always love me and guide my path
with a quiet, gentle voice.
I remember well the day I vowed
to make You my first choice.
I thank You, Jesus, for being with me
through challenges, great and small.
I know I'm Yours forever now ...
even when I fall.

I worship You with song and prayer;
grateful You hold me tight.
May my life on earth reflect to all
Your amazing, perfect Light.

God's Care

Thank You for Your love, Lord;
thank You for Your care.
I feel Your protective hand
and I know You're always there.

I fail and trip and stumble
in my feeble, earthly ways.
I know You'll never leave me ...
You'll protect me all my days.

Honour

In all I do and all I say ...
in all I think and all I pray,
I ask You, Jesus, to keep me true
as I live to honour You.

You died for me on the cross;
You took my sin and shame.
You promised me eternal life
before I spoke Your name

I'm Your child; I know I'm blessed,
You've never left my side.
The peace and comfort that I feel
can never be denied

GOD'S PROTECTION

Peace

Dear Lord, another day has passed ...
each minute You were near.
I pray our world will be at peace,
an end to pain and fear.

You guide my steps all day long
and keep me free from harm.
I know You want the best for me,
that knowledge gives me calm.

I love You, Lord, I trust in You ...
I give You all the praise.
You're the foundation of my life
whom I'll honour all my days.

You bless me undeservedly
in everything I do.
When I slip up, You set me right ...
You never fail, thank You.

I feel Your touch and know You're here,
serenity floods my soul.
My path with You is straight and clear ...
thank You that I'm now whole.

GOD'S PURPOSE

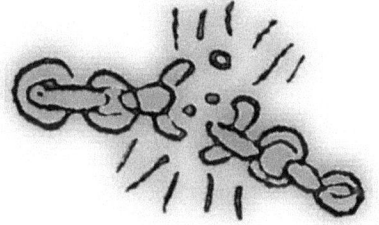

GOD'S PURPOSE

Understanding

When I first understood
my purpose here on earth,
my world changed and opened up;
I experienced my re-birth.

From Heaven You called and changed me ...
with You I will achieve
true peace and fruitfulness in life ...
praise God, I now believe!

Jesus, as Your children
we know Your powerful ways.
We hear Your words of comfort
which help in challenging days.

We know the Holy Spirit works
to achieve Your awesome plan.
We'll spread the blessings, love and Words
from our Saviour, The Lamb.

Your Plan

Darkness, sadness, fear and doubt
  flood over all this earth.
Joy and faith and hope and light
  will bring wondrous rebirth.

You have planned these darker times
  for us on earth, we know.
Please help us to teach the blind
  so their love for You may grow.

Our trust in You will never fail ...
  we understand God's plan.
We need to spread Your Gospel to
  every woman, child and man.

We're ready, Lord, to hear Your voice ...
  for You our lamps are lit.
We're ready, Lord, to follow You
  and, for evermore, submit.

Darkness, sadness, fear and doubt
  flood over all this earth.
Joy and faith and hope and light
  Will bring wondrous rebirth.

God's Purpose

The Holy Spirit

Come, Holy Spirit, come ...
please come and hold me tight.
Fill me again, renew my heart
so I can spread Your light.

Come, Holy Spirit, come ...
please heal my broken soul.
Without You I am nothing
but Your presence makes me whole.

Come, Holy Spirit, come ...
and lead me in Your way.
Please hold my hand, don't let me go ...
I don't ever want to stray.

Come, Holy Spirit, come ...
witness my human plan
which is to live for You alone ...
and now I know I can.

Come, Holy Spirit, come ...
please convict me when I'm wrong.
I love to hear Your precious word
and praise You with my song.

Come, Holy Spirit, come ...
please empower me
to focus just on You, Jesus,
the One I want to see.

Possessions

Dear God, help me to understand
nothing on earth is mine.
My Children, who are loaned to me,
are fruit from You, The Vine.

Help me to be generous
with material things ... and 'stuff'.
May I always be content because
I know I have enough.

I don't need the best or latest ...
it's purely earthly greed.
All I have is Yours, I know
You give me all I need.

May I concentrate on giving
to build my treasure in Heaven ...
and then I'll know completion ...
Your perfect Number 7.

GOD'S PURPOSE

Our Greatest Aim

Your gentle voice reminds us that we must spread Your Word.
For some of us it's daunting ... Your Gospel must be heard.

You are the God of comfort to all who are in pain.
Should complacency creep in You'll prompt us once again.

We venture out to city streets and meet those who are not saved.
Some are grateful ... others not ... for the path that Jesus paved.

As His children, we must share the wonders of His being.
When others choose to follow Him transformation we'll be seeing.

Rejection? No-one likes that much but we smile and try once more.
When we find a receptive soul, lives change and our hearts soar.

May we stop being complacent, may we declare Your Name.
To spread the Gospel and Your love must be our greatest aim.

Here is my Heart, Lord

Here is my heart, Lord, speak all that is true.
I'm here and listening in obedience to You.

Here is my heart, Lord, for years it was lost.
My sins now forgiven ... Your life was the cost.

Here is my heart, Lord, overflowing with praise.
You've lovingly taught me to walk in Your ways.

Here is my heart, Lord, full of gratitude.
You've changed my life's path and I'm now renewed.

Here is my heart, Lord, without You I drift.
I welcome Your promptings, to me they're a gift.

Here is my heart, Lord; here is my soul.
Here is my everything ... with You I am whole.

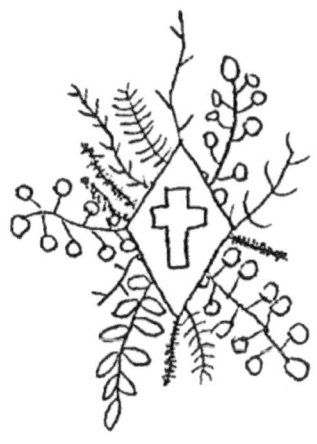

PRAYER & ENCOURAGEMENT

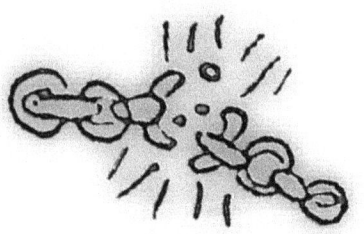

Opening Prayer

We thank You that we're gathered here
and pray for those who are elsewhere.
We want to listen, learn, discuss
and do all that You ask of us.

You've blessed us all and we thank You, Lord.
We praise and love You with one accord.
Father, we ask of You today
that in our lives You have Your way.

We're here to study Your living word ...
don't let our focus become blurred.
Please bless this special time we share ...
this is, today, my opening prayer.

A Close Friend has Died

The last few weeks were challenging ...
but now you rest in peace.
God's Angels welcome you in Heaven
and our memories will not cease.

We stand together in this Church
to remember you today.
The good and bad times, laughs and tears
will never go away.

These last few weeks were challenging
before God took you home.
Now He is yours and you are His ...
you'll never be alone.

Reach Out

I aim to share God's wondrous gifts
with others, every day.
A smile, supportive hug or text ...
that's become my way.

I know we all have challenges
and dark thoughts hang around.
Whilst friends can be supportive
in Jesus our truth is found.

We should always look to Heaven
for the answers we pursue ...
but hearing from a loving friend
can lift our spirits, too.

So, can we all reach out in love
to brighten someone's day?
May a smile, supportive hug or text
also become your way.

PRAYER & ENCOURAGEMENT

Encouraging Others

Shine through me, reveal Your love
to those who do not see.
Use me any way You wish
to touch them ... as You touched me.

May I be Your messenger
for those who've lost their way.
Jesus, I praise and honour You
and love You more each day.

I ask for Your forgiveness
as I confess my sin.
The freedom that I've found in You
comes from my soul, within.

I want the world to know Your truth ...
that on the cross You died.
May I live in obedience to You
and help others, far and wide.

I Want...

I want to be Your presence
everywhere I go ...
to be loving and humble
so Your goodness I can show.

I want to encourage others
seven days a week ...
to support, in every circumstance,
with every word I speak.

I want to tell the sceptics
You are merciful and just.
Your love and goodness transform lives,
and in You they can trust.

I want to share the gospel
with everyone in need.
Guide me to those who don't know You ...
so I may plant Your seed.

I want to love and honour You
with everything I am.
I dedicate my life to You ...
The Lion and The Lamb.

Fruits of The Holy Spirit

Lord, I pray You're with me
in all I say and do.
I ask You now to guide my steps
in ways which honour You.
I know I'm often not
the Christian I want to be ...
Jesus, open up my eyes
so my shortfalls I can see.

I ask for help to unlock my soul
from gossip and idle chatter;
may I only hear the Godly
principles which matter.
Most of all, please guard may heart
from worldly thoughts and ways ...
Convict me, Holy Spirit,
so my heart no longer strays.

Lord, I'm Your child, You love me
and I'm blessed beyond compare;
may I love others that same way
so they understand I care.

And may all the words I speak
be pure and good and true ...
my soul is overflowing
with praise and love for You.
Patience and humility,
those gifts today are rare
May my arrogance and pride be gone ...
this is my fervent prayer.
May The Holy Spirit's fruit in me
be recognised by all
so they turn to You, dear Jesus,
and on Your Name they call.

Send Me

May I reflect Your awesome grace
to those who do not see.
Use me in any way You wish
to touch others ... as You touched me.

I'll be Your vessel, willingly,
for those who've lost their way.
Lord, I love and honour You
more and more each day.

May I shine with peace and love,
gentleness and self-control.
May those I touch receive Your light
as truth unchains their soul.

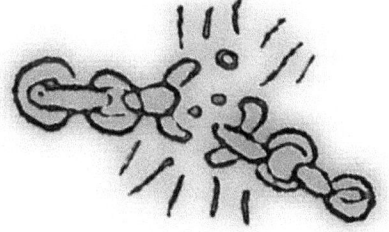

A Mother's Love

A part of me has died inside
but my candle flickers on.
I love him and I want him near ...
Jesus, please guide my Son.

You know how much I love my child
but he has gone awry.
My prayer to You ... please save him
and do not pass him by.

May he one day return to us
so we can be close again.
Until that time please keep him safe ...
Love always and ... Amen.

A Lost Son

I love you, but don't know you;
that's not how I want to live.
I love you, but we're strangers ...
you know that I'll forgive.

Every Day

Every day my heart feels heavier;
every day my sorrow grows,
but I believe that God will change you ...
when? Only He knows.

Every day I want to hug you;
every day to hear your voice.
I believe God's working in you
and when He's done we'll all rejoice.

Every day my eyes get teary;
every day I'm wondering
how you are and what you're doing ...
the emptiness is thundering.

Every day I want to phone you;
every day to see your face.
I know that it's God's plan to save you
through His mercy and His grace.

GRIEF

Different Paths

I'd love to see you often
but doubt that'll ever be.
The ways our lives unfolded
show there's little interest in me.

As children, we were guided
to know and love the Lord.
Our parents worshipped Jesus
and lived strictly by His Word.

We both left our Christian paths
but then God called me back.
I wish you'd hear my cry to you
and join me on His track.

When I talk about the faith,
which we shared in our youth,
I feel mocked for my belief ...
but why? You know the truth!

I love you and admire you
as I reminisce our past.
You're my wonderful big Brother
and my love will always last.

REFLECTIONS

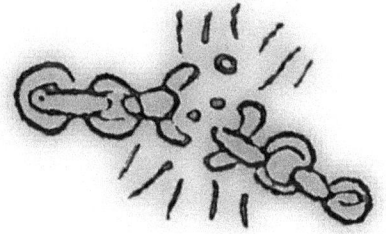

The Past

Thank You for the challenges
I've conquered in my life.
The heartaches of earlier years
when a young mum and wife.

Those years were a real nightmare
because I didn't know You then.
I just survived them on my own …
praise God I'm born again.

I'm glad I struggled through those years …
without them I wouldn't know
how to comfort others when
through painful times they go.

I am renewed, I'm happy now …
Your plan is crystal clear.
I trust You, Jesus, totally …
You've taken all my fear.

Jesus truly understands
and guides me day and night.
Without Him, life is darkness and
knowing Him is Light.

Repentance

I've chosen paths which were unwise ...
You've saved me constantly.
My selfish ways, desires and thoughts
with contrition I now see.

I'm in the winter of my life
and know that I am blessed.
Every day I'll live for You
until I'm laid to rest.

GRATITUDE

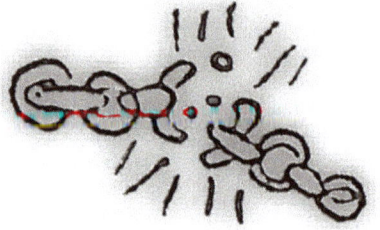

My Cup

My cup is overflowing
with the love poured over me.
Jesus, I now live for You
and that's why I am free.

My cup is overflowing
now that I'm forgiven.
I honour and obey Your call
and worship You in Heaven,

My cup is overflowing
with Your abundant grace.
I hear Your quiet conviction
and can almost see Your face.

My cup is overflowing
with the patience that You show.
I trip and stumble constantly
but You never let me go.

My cup is overflowing
with every blessing from Your hand.
My heart is filled with gratitude
and with You I'll always stand.

Providence

Our world is filled with anger, pain,
selfishness and greed.
Lord, as Your children we understand
that You are all we need.

Your never-ending providence
fills us every day.
Your continued love and presence
guides us in every way.

Sometimes I struggle to forgive
but Your Word says I must...
and, when I do, Your quiet voice
confirms it's You I trust.

I thank You that I hear Your voice
so clearly in my soul.
Jesus, I'm anchored in Your Word
as You gradually make me whole.

God's Grace

I stand before You, Loving God;
I feel remorse and shame.
Only for Your amazing grace
can I call upon Your name.

I believed I was unworthy
to receive Your powerful gifts;
but I feel them every morning
and my spirit always lifts.

Dear Jesus, I am drowning in
the blessings I've received.
The changes You've made in my life
I could never have believed.

I thank You, Lord, with all my heart
for this Christian path I tread.
You provide all I need and want ...
Your amazing daily bread.

GRATITUDE

My Guide

God, I am in awe of You ...
my Heavenly Guide in all I do.
You have blessed me all my years,
in happy times, in fears and tears.
I thank You that I am Your child ...
now loving You, no longer wild.
I honour You, now You're my Lord ...
my Saviour, Teacher, Father God.

To Know You

To know You is to love You ...
to honour and obey.
Watch over me and guide my steps,
I want to live Your way.

To know You is to praise You
with prayer, thanks and song.
Your victory on the cross tells me
to You I now belong.

To know You is to understand
that I am now forgiven.
My life transformed, I'm truly blessed
by my Saviour, in Heaven.

Perfect Match

You've honoured God, your Saviour,
for many, many years.
He's answered prayer, He's blessed you both
and held you through your fears.

I see the love between you ...
it's clearly in your eyes.
You were each led to your perfect match ...
to me that's no surprise.

I feel the bond between you ...
the ways you care and smile.
Your happiness in tangible, but
that's always been your style.

I know Jesus is with you ...
you chose to walk His path.
Your loving, giving lifestyles
have not incurred His wrath.

You've both received so many gifts ...
clearly from above.
Your marriage ... a perfect witness
for God's unrivalled love.

Grand Children

I have lived an awesome life
and now look on to see
my beautiful Grand Daughters ...
who mean the world to me!

Grand children are the precious gift
received in my later years.
They transformed my life in every way ...
my eyes fill with proud tears.

They're strong in Christ, they're caring
in every Christian way.
I can't see them ever changing ...
I know with God they'll stay.

I've been close to them since birth
and blessed to see them grow
from tiny tots to Christian teens ...
oh, where did those years go?

Our childhoods were so different
and our challenges worlds apart.
I learn from them, they hear my story;
we chat, heart to heart.

The beauty of these young ladies
comes from their faith and love
for Jesus, who fits perfectly,
just like a hand and glove.

Broken Chains

Our world is changing rapidly ...
I don't like some things I see.
I try to blend my traditional past
with the modern Nanna, me!

Whatever happens, we all know
Jesus is our only goal.
Keep trusting Him, obey His Word
because He is in control.

I treasure all my memories;
I'm filled with joy and pride.
I'll adore and bless my Grand Daughters
'till with Jesus I abide.

GOD'S VICTORY

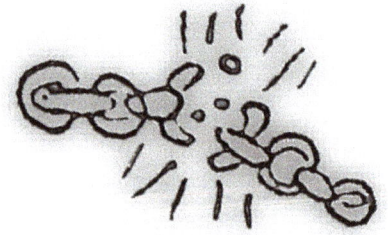

Standing in His Victory

Whatever my situation You know just what to do.
I close my eyes and call Your name ... You always guide me through.

I listen to Your teaching as I fight my angst and pain.
When I live in Your obedience Your peace floods me again.

God's Mercy

Lord, I seek Your guidance and help, in every way.
I clearly see Your path for me yet sadly I still stray.

You hold my hand so lovingly but I sometimes let You go.
I sin ... You catch me in Your arms; Your love for me You show.

Forgiveness is a precious gift and one I don't deserve.
Please help me to be obedient ... it's You I want to serve.

I Surrender

May I surrender to You, Lord,
when I sit with You in prayer.
I feel the comfort of Your love
and know You're always there.

May I surrender to You, Lord,
in all I do and say.
I live to honour You alone
when I awake each day,

May I surrender to You, Lord,
until You call me home.
Jesus, when I leave this world
I'll bow down at Your throne.

I'll praise You and adore You
for all eternity.
I'll see Your face and know, for sure,
nothing again can hurt me.

My Lord and Saviour

You are my Lord and Saviour ...
You've never let me down.
It's hard for me to fathom because
I don't deserve that crown.

You are my Lord and Saviour ...
who guides me night and day.
I feel You close, I hear Your voice,
You always light my way.

You are my Lord and Saviour ...
You convict me when I sin.
I ask for Your forgiveness and
Your healing floods within.

You are my Lord and Saviour
whom I trust and obey.
My daily prayer to You is that
in me, You have Your way.

Looking Back

You've blessed me, undeservedly,
all my days on earth.
But when You left the 99
I understood my worth.

Since I was young, You've held me
and never let me go.
I finally felt Your wondrous love ...
I know I was very slow.

I love You, Jesus; I praise You
for Your goodness and Your grace.
You paid for my sin and shame
and humbly took my place.

The way we humans live today
suggests the end is nigh.
I'm ready, Lord, to see Your face
and be with You on high.

www.ingramcontent.com/pod-product-compliance
Lightning Source LLC
Chambersburg PA
CBHW051540010526
44107CB00064B/2798